AUG    2011

DISCARD

PROPERTY OF C L P L

# NIGHTMARE PLAGUES

# BUBONIC PLAGUE
## The Black Death!

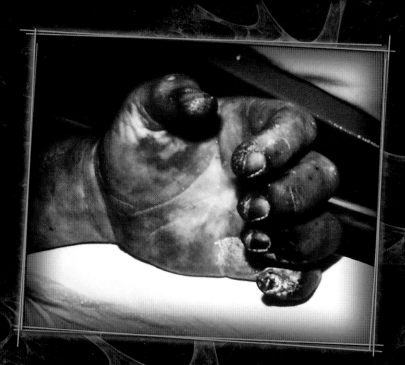

## by Stephen Person

Consultant: Susan Straley, Ph.D.
Microbiologist and Plague Researcher
University of Kentucky
Lexington, Kentucky

## BEARPORT
PUBLISHING

New York, New York

# Credits

Cover and Title Page, Courtesy of The Centers for Disease Control and Prevention/Dr. Jack Poland; 4, © The Bancroft Library. University of California, Berkeley; 5T, Courtesy of The Centers for Disease Control and Prevention; 5B, © Robert Clay/Alamy; 6, Courtesy of The Library of Congress ; 7T, © The Bancroft Library. University of California, Berkeley; 7B, © Gridley Herald, November 12 1924/Newspaper Archive; 8T, © Science and Society/SuperStock; 8B, © Eye of Science/Photo Researchers, Inc.; 9T, © Courtesy of The Centers for Disease Control and Prevention; 9B, © Stephen Dalton/NHPA/Photoshot; 10, © George Bernard/NHPA/Photoshot; 11, © Alinari Archives/The Image Works; 12, © Costume designed to protect doctors from the plague, 1720 (w/c on paper), French School, (18th century)/Bibliotheque Nationale, Paris, France/Archives Charmet/The Bridgeman Art Library International; 14, © RIA Novosti/Alamy; 15T, © Classic Image/Alamy; 15B, © Sergey Sorokin; 16L, © Siège d'Auberoche (1345)/Bibliothèque Nationale de France; 16R, © Lourens Smak/Alamy; 17, © SuperStock; 18, © De Agostini/SuperStock; 19T, © The Art Archive/SuperStock; 19B, Courtesy of The Centers for Disease Control and Prevention; 20L, © Mary Evans Picture Library/Alamy; 20R, © Mary Evans Picture Library/Alamy; 21, © Wellcome Library, London; 22, © Gianni Dagli Orti/The Art Archive/Alamy; 23, © Science Photo Library/Photo Researchers, Inc.; 24, © Felidae Conservation Fund; 25, © Felidae Conservation Fund; 27, © Ting-Li Wang/The New York Times/Redux; 28, © Paris Pierce/Alamy; 29, © cmsbiology/Newscom; 31, © Maslov Dmitry/Shutterstock.

Publisher: Kenn Goin
Senior Editor: Lisa Wiseman
Creative Director: Spencer Brinker
Design: Dawn Beard Creative
Photo Researcher: Daniella Nilva

*Library of Congress Cataloging-in-Publication Data*

Person, Stephen.
  Bubonic plague : the black death! / by Stephen Person.
    p. cm. — (Nightmare plagues)
  Includes bibliographical references and index.
  ISBN-13: 978-1-936088-03-4 (library binding)
  ISBN-10: 1-936088-03-7 (library binding)
  1. Plague—Juvenile literature. 2. Black Death—Juvenile literature. I. Title.
  RA644.P7P367 2011
  614.5'732—dc22
                    2010008028

Copyright © 2011 Bearport Publishing Company, Inc. All rights reserved. No part of this publication may be reproduced in whole or in part, stored in a retrieval system, or transmitted in any form or by any means, electronic, mechanical, photocopying, recording, or otherwise, without written permission from the publisher.

For more information, write to Bearport Publishing Company, Inc., 101 Fifth Avenue, Suite 6R, New York, New York 10003. Printed in the United States of America in North Mankato, Minnesota.

062010
042110CGC

10 9 8 7 6 5 4 3 2 1

# Contents

# A Mysterious Killer

It was a hot day in Los Angeles, California, in September 1924. Jesus Lajun (hay-SOOS la-HOON) noticed a terrible smell coming from somewhere in his house. He went down to the basement and spotted the source. It was a dead, rotting rat. Not thinking much of it, Lajun picked up the rat and tossed it in the trash.

Jesus Lajun and his family lived in a house like this one on Clara Street near downtown Los Angeles.

Days later, Lajun came down with a fever along with muscle pain and headaches. Then he noticed a lump on his thigh. It was the size of an egg and very painful. About a week later, he started coughing up blood. Within three days, he was dead.

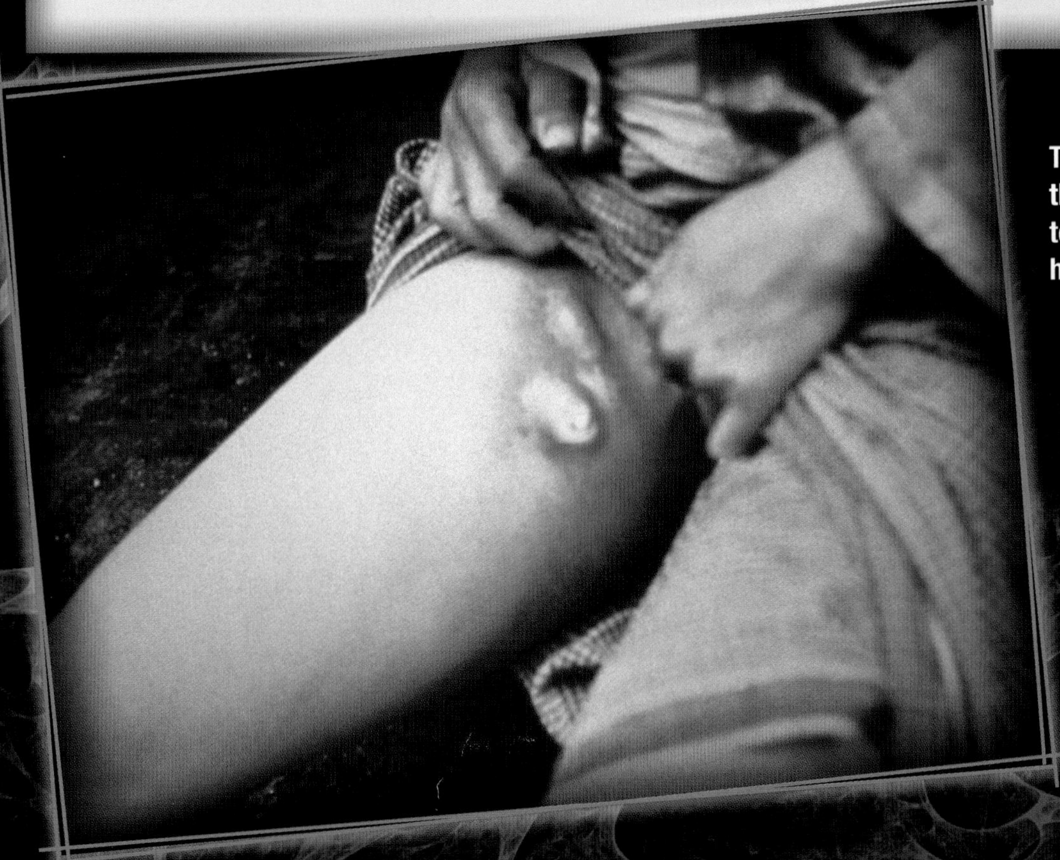

The lump on Lajun's thigh looked similar to the ones shown here.

Lajun found a dead rat in his basement.

At first, doctors had no idea what had killed Jesus Lajun. They thought it might have been meningitis or pneumonia. Both of these illnesses cause **symptoms** similar to the ones that Lajun was experiencing.

# Plague Hits Los Angeles

Within days of Lajun getting sick, his teenage daughter caught the same strange illness and died a week later. Then several neighbors became sick and died. So did the ambulance driver who had taken them to the hospital. Even the priest who had performed their funerals got sick and died. As the mysterious killer continued to spread, panic ripped through Los Angeles.

In 1924, Los Angeles was a growing city of about 600,000 people.

At a city hospital, a doctor studied a sample of blood from one of the victims. He was shocked by what he saw under the microscope. The killer disease was **plague**. Since plague is very **contagious**, city officials quickly **quarantined** the entire neighborhood where the disease was found. No one was allowed to leave the area. Thanks to the quarantine, the disease, which had hit in September, stopped spreading by the middle of November.

There was no cure for plague in the 1920s. Doctors studied the disease, in labs such as this one in Los Angeles, in order to find a treatment for this contagious killer.

Newspaper reports of plague spread fear in the 1920s.

L. A. ON GUARD AGAINST ENTRY OF NEW PLAGUE

Two Cases of Suspected

A total of 37 people died of plague in Los Angeles in 1924. This was the last large **outbreak** of plague in an American city.

# A Tale of Rats and Fleas

So just how did Jesus Lajun become infected with plague? It all started with the dead rat that he innocently threw away. In the late 1800s, researchers discovered that plague is caused by a type of **bacteria** called *Yersinia pestis*. The bacteria live in the bodies of **fleas** that normally make their home in the fur of rats and other rodents.

In the early 1900s, many cities paid people to set traps to kill rats and other rodents. Killing the rodents slowed the spread of plague.

A close-up view of plague bacteria—
*Yersinia pestis*

Fleas live on rats so they can feed on their blood. When a plague-infected flea bites a rat, it spreads plague to the animal. When a rat dies from the disease, the fleas need a new source of food. So they jump to another rat. If there are no more live rats, fleas sometimes jump to humans.

Doctors suspect that the rat in Lajun's basement had died of plague. When Lajun picked it up, plague-carrying fleas jumped onto his skin and bit him.

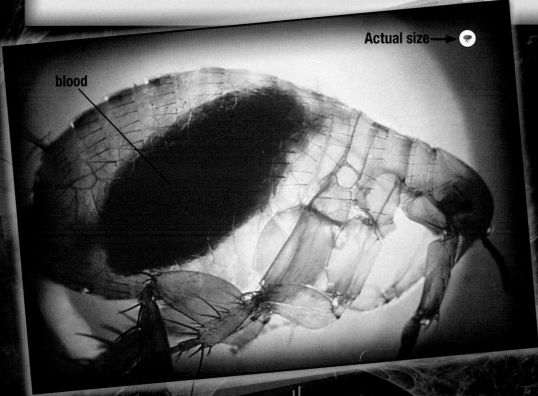

Actual size ➔

blood

This close-up photo shows a flea with a belly full of blood.

Fleas can live up to two weeks without a human or animal **host**. They are sometimes found in clothing, waiting for a new host to pass by.

A single rat can have hundreds of disease-carrying fleas on its body.

9

# Bubonic Plague

Fleas infected with plague carry the bacteria in their **digestive systems**. When they bite a human, the bacteria are released into the human's body and travel to the **lymph nodes**.

A flea biting a human

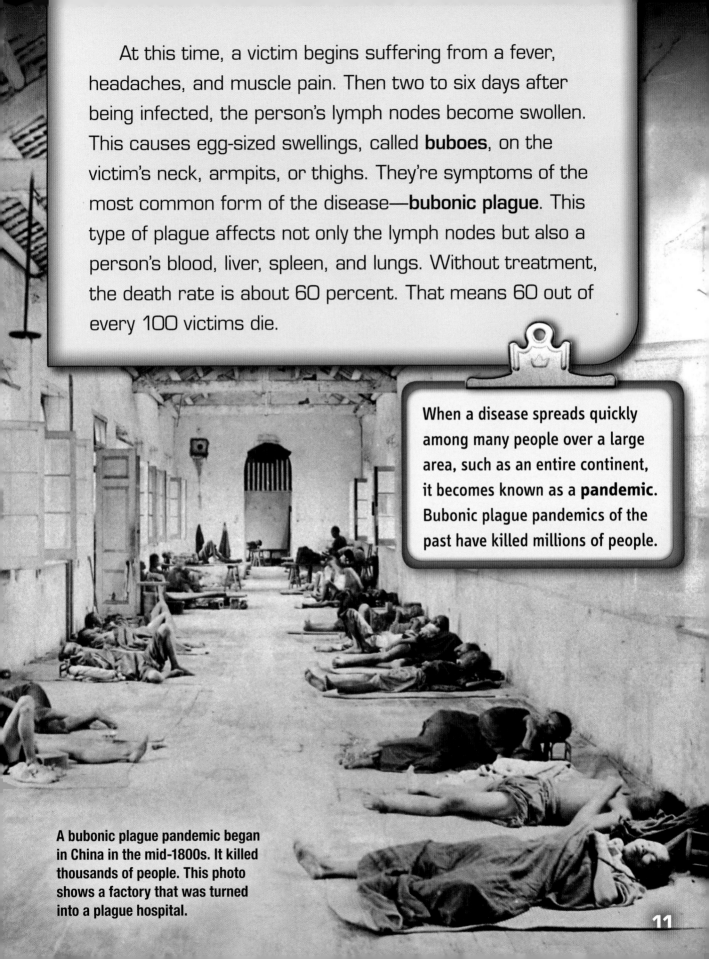

At this time, a victim begins suffering from a fever, headaches, and muscle pain. Then two to six days after being infected, the person's lymph nodes become swollen. This causes egg-sized swellings, called **buboes**, on the victim's neck, armpits, or thighs. They're symptoms of the most common form of the disease—**bubonic plague**. This type of plague affects not only the lymph nodes but also a person's blood, liver, spleen, and lungs. Without treatment, the death rate is about 60 percent. That means 60 out of every 100 victims die.

When a disease spreads quickly among many people over a large area, such as an entire continent, it becomes known as a **pandemic**. Bubonic plague pandemics of the past have killed millions of people.

A bubonic plague pandemic began in China in the mid-1800s. It killed thousands of people. This photo shows a factory that was turned into a plague hospital.

# Three Ways to Die

There are two other types of plague that a person can develop besides bubonic—**pneumonic plague** and **septicemic plague**. The type depends on how the bacteria enter a person's body and where they settle.

Pneumonic plague occurs when the plague bacteria settle in the lungs. This can happen in one of two ways. First, a person can inhale the bacteria from someone suffering from the disease. Second, the disease may spread to the lungs in a person who has bubonic plague that's left untreated. Either way, the lungs fill with fluid and violent coughing follows. After growing in the lungs, the bacteria eventually enter the bloodstream and spread to the spleen and liver. Without quick treatment, pneumonic plague can kill in just a few days. The death rate is about 95 percent. Doctors believe that Jesus Lajun died after his bubonic plague spread to his lungs and became pneumonic plague.

Hundreds of years ago, doctors didn't know what caused plague to spread. They hoped that by covering their bodies with gloves, long robes, and masks they would be protected against the disease.

Just like bubonic plague, septicemic plague occurs through a fleabite. However, the bacteria don't travel to the lymph nodes, so buboes don't form. Instead, the bacteria go directly into the blood and travel to the liver, spleen, and even the lungs. People who have bubonic or pneumonic plague and are not receiving treatment can develop this form of the disease as well. This is the most deadly type of plague, with a 100 percent death rate.

| Form of Plague | Parts of Body Affected | Symptoms | How It Spreads | Death Rate, Without Treatment |
|---|---|---|---|---|
| Bubonic | the lymph nodes, the blood, the liver, the spleen, and the lungs | fever; muscle pain; egg-sized buboes on thighs, neck, or underarms; bleeding under the skin | fleabites | 60% |
| Pneumonic | the lungs, the blood, the liver, and the spleen | fever, trouble breathing, bloody cough, bleeding under the skin | inhaling bacteria from a victim's coughs or sneezes; can also develop in untreated bubonic plague victims | 95% |
| Septicemic | the blood, the liver, the spleen, and the lungs | same as bubonic plague but without buboes | fleabites; can also develop in an untreated bubonic or pneumonic plague victim | 100% |

The form of plague a victim gets depends on how the bacteria enter the person's body and where they settle once inside.

Pneumonic plague is the most contagious form of the disease. It can travel from person to person on the droplets of **saliva** in victims' coughs and sneezes. A person can catch pneumonic plague by breathing in plague bacteria floating in the air.

# The Worst Pandemic

While plague spread terror across Los Angeles in the 1920s, it was nothing compared to what it did to Europe in the 1300s. In 1347, the bubonic plague entered eastern Europe at the **port** city of Caffa on the Black Sea. Caffa, a city protected by stone walls, was located in what is now the country of Ukraine.

A painting of what Caffa looked like in the 1300s

A Turkish army was battling Italian soldiers for control of Caffa. With the Italians inside, the Turks surrounded the city. They seemed sure to win the fight—until something strange happened. Many soldiers began to have aches and fevers. Soon, buboes formed on their bodies. Within a week of the symptoms' onset, many of them were dead.

Scientists believe this pandemic of bubonic plague began in Asia, probably in China's Gobi Desert in the 1320s. From there, it spread east and west as people traveled along **trade routes**. This is how it reached eastern Europe.

When attacking a walled city such as Caffa, soldiers often used ladders to climb over the walls to get inside.

Caffa is now called Feodosiya (*fay*-ah-DOH-see-ah). This seaside town is popular with tourists. Parts of Caffa's walls still stand today.

# Bodies from the Sky

The terrified Turks had no idea what was killing them. However, they hoped they could spread the strange disease to their enemies. Using **catapults**, the surviving Turks shot the bodies of dead soldiers over the walls surrounding Caffa. The bodies sailed into the city and landed on the ground.

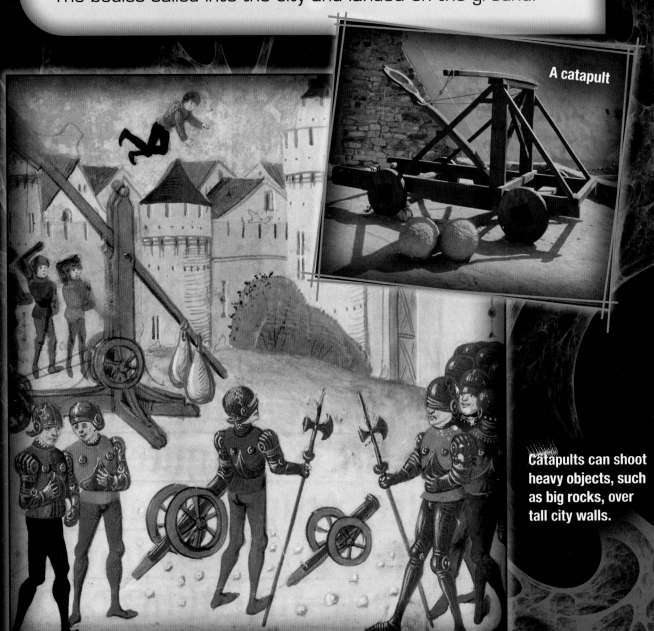

A catapult

Catapults can shoot heavy objects, such as big rocks, over tall city walls.

Italian soldiers dragged the bodies off the streets. As they did, the plague bacteria got onto their hands and other body parts. Within days, the Italians began dying quick and horrible deaths. The Turks' plan had worked.

The survivors inside Caffa panicked. They ran to their ships, and sailed for home. They hoped to get away from the killer disease. Instead, they unknowingly took it with them.

Traders traveling by ship helped spread the disease in the 1300s. As ships sailed from port to port, sailors—and rats on the ships—often brought contagious diseases along with them.

# Black Death Batters Europe

Many of the Italians who fled Caffa grew sick and died before their ships reached Italy. Nonetheless, after a few months at sea, several ships arrived in Messina, a town on the Italian island of Sicily. When the soldiers went ashore, they unknowingly began to spread plague through the town. Many of these men began to die. Soon, some of the citizens of Messina starting dying, too. Those who were healthy enough fled to the **mainland** of Italy. Without knowing it, however, they took plague-carrying fleas with them. Soon, people in Italy began dying from the disease as well.

## The Route from Caffa to Messina

The city of Messina is located on the Straits of Messina. Just two miles (3.2 km) wide, this waterway separates Sicily from the mainland of Italy.

The trip from Caffa to Messina was more than 1,000 miles (1,609 km).

From Italy, plague spread across Europe. It reached France early in 1348. From France, fleas, rats, and people carried the disease north, east, and west. "We are struck with terror," said one man in England before the disease arrived. People had heard about the deadly plague and knew it was coming. Yet, they could do nothing to stop it.

This painting shows plague victims in a market square in Italy. Many people who took care of the sick soon became sick themselves.

Plague can cause bleeding under the skin, which results in dark spots. This may be why some people began calling the disease the Black Death.

A person with plague whose fingers are bleeding under the skin

# Counting the Dead

So many people in Europe fell ill from plague during the 1300s that life came to a stop. Shops were closed. Churches were left half built. Crops rotted in the fields. Farm animals wandered from village to village. Every day, people pulled carts piled with dead bodies through the streets. "There were hardly enough people left alive to bury the dead," said a man in England.

By 1351, plague had wiped out nearly half the people in major cities in Europe such as Florence, Paris, and London.

Many people burned down their homes. They thought this would help get rid of plague. It didn't, but it did kill the fleas.

Trade between cities and nations slowed to a crawl. While this was bad for businesses, it did help stop the spread of the disease. By 1352, the worst was finally over. Historians believe that about 25 million people died of plague in Europe between 1347 and 1352. That was about one third of its entire **population**. The pandemic also killed millions in Asia and Africa.

In order to help keep bubonic plague out of cities and towns, doctors would examine sailors before they were allowed to leave their ships to come ashore. This practice was common for hundreds of years as shown in this drawing from the 1900s.

Seventy-five million people had been living in Europe when the disease struck in 1347. After the pandemic, it took more than 200 years for Europe's population to reach that number again.

# Treatment

For many centuries, doctors had no idea how to treat plague victims. Some doctors tried slicing open the buboes to let the fluid flow out. They hoped this would cause the disease to flow out as well. Other doctors believed that causing patients to sweat or bleed might force the disease to leave their bodies. However, none of these treatments had any effect on the plague bacteria.

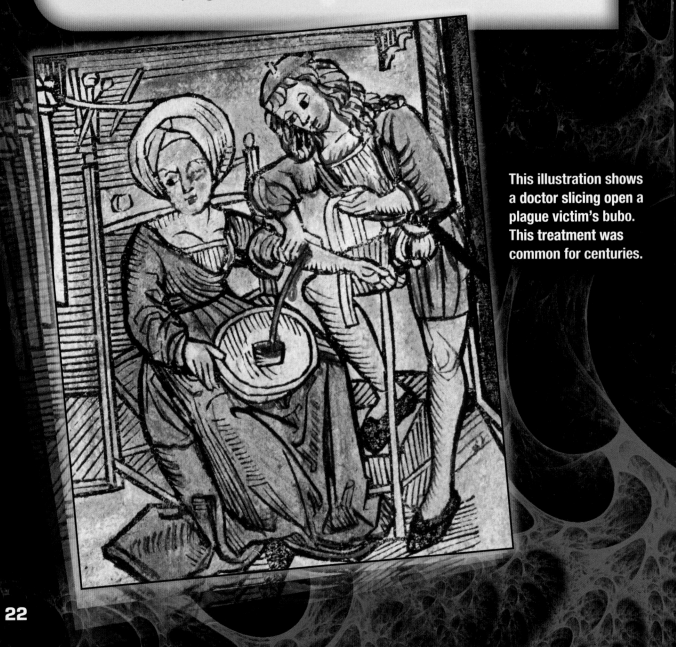

This illustration shows a doctor slicing open a plague victim's bubo. This treatment was common for centuries.

Finally, in the 1940s, doctors developed medicines called **antibiotics**. The antibiotics kill bacteria that cause plague and many other diseases. If taken early on, these medicines are effective in curing victims of plague.

Antibiotics have not only helped victims with bubonic plague. They have also saved the lives of many people who were ill with other diseases, such as meningitis, pneumonia, tuberculosis, and scarlet fever. Today doctors still prescribe antibiotics to treat diseases caused by bacteria.

Doctors studied the bodies of rats that died during a bubonic plague outbreak in New Orleans in 1914. This type of research led to the discovery of medicines effective in treating the disease.

# Plague Strikes Again!

In 2007, about 660 years after the start of the worst plague pandemic in history, a wildlife **biologist** named Eric York was walking in Arizona's Grand Canyon National Park. He spotted a dead mountain lion. The lion's nose had been bleeding. There were no other signs of illness or injury, though. Eric was curious to find out why the lion died, so he took the body to his home.

Eric York worked for the National Park Service studying mountain lions.

On October 27, Eric cut the body open and searched for clues. On October 30, he began suffering from fever and body aches. Three days later, Eric was found dead on his couch. Tests showed that he died of pneumonic plague. Panic spread across the Grand Canyon area.

After examining the mountain lion, doctors determined that plague had killed the animal. They concluded that when Eric cut the body open, he must have breathed in plague bacteria.

Eric York was just 37 years old when he died.

# Plague Lives On

Luckily, this wasn't the start of another plague outbreak. Doctors were prepared with modern medicine and quickly tracked down every person Eric had come in contact with after handling the lion. All 49 people were treated with antibiotics. No one developed plague. This time, the disease had been wiped out before it could spread.

## Reported Cases of Plague

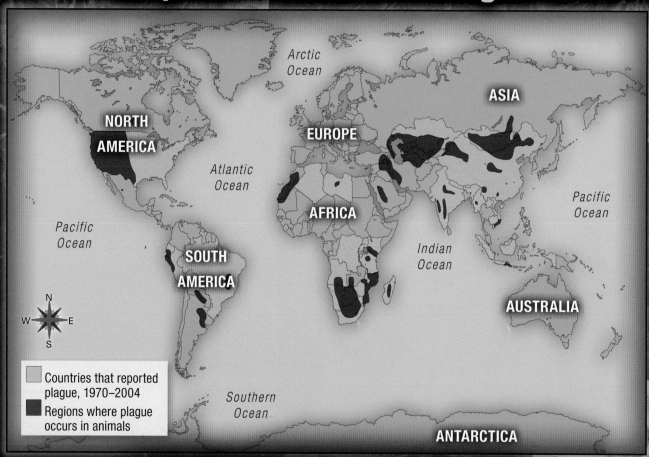

Countries that reported plague, 1970–2004

Regions where plague occurs in animals

Plague is still widespread, though it no longer threatens Europe.

When used quickly, modern medicines are very effective in curing this disease. Yet a small number of people are still getting plague. About 13 people get the disease every year in the United States. Around the world, 1,000 to 3,000 cases are reported each year. Hopefully, a major plague pandemic will never terrify the world again.

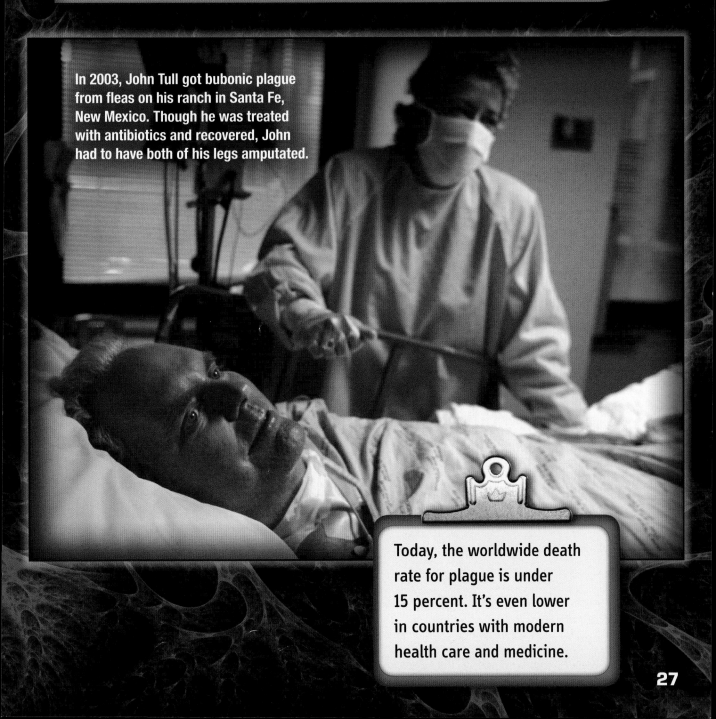

In 2003, John Tull got bubonic plague from fleas on his ranch in Santa Fe, New Mexico. Though he was treated with antibiotics and recovered, John had to have both of his legs amputated.

Today, the worldwide death rate for plague is under 15 percent. It's even lower in countries with modern health care and medicine.

# Other Famous Plague Pandemics

Over the past 1,500 years, *Yersinia pestis* bacteria have caused several major plague pandemics, killing millions of people.

## The Plague of Justinian

- This pandemic was named for Justinian, the leader of the Byzantine Empire. At the time the plague struck, he ruled many areas, including Turkey and parts of Italy, North Africa, and Spain.

- The outbreak is believed to have begun in Egypt, a country in Africa, in about 542 B.C. Trading ships then carried plague to cities bordering the Mediterranean Sea.

- The pandemic, which lasted for about 50 years, killed millions of people.

## The Third Pandemic

- The Plague of Justinian was the first plague pandemic recorded in history. The second was called the Black Death, which hit Europe in the 1300s. Another plague pandemic in the 1800s became known as the Third Pandemic.

- The Third Pandemic began in China in the 1850s and spread across much of the world, killing more than 10 million people by 1900.

- Plague reached the western United States during this pandemic. It probably arrived first in a San Francisco port in 1900.

- This was the last major pandemic of bubonic plague.

During the worst of the Plague of Justinian, the pandemic killed about 10,000 people a day in the Byzantine capital of Constantinople, now called Istanbul, in the country of Turkey. Nearly half the city's population was wiped out.

# Bubonic Plague Facts

During the 1300s, people thought plague might be caused by bad diets or polluted air. It was not until the 1890s that doctors discovered the bacteria that cause plague. Here are some other facts about bubonic plague.

## Plague Prevention

- Fleas carrying plague still live on wild rodents in many parts of the world, including the western United States. Contact with rodents in these areas should be avoided.

- People living in areas where plague exists should be especially careful to make sure their pets don't have fleas.

- If large numbers of rodents die suddenly, this should be reported to health officials. It may be a sign that plague is spreading among the animals.

- Anyone who suspects he or she may have been near an infected animal or flea should seek medical help right away.

## What to Do

- People who have symptoms of plague— such as buboes and a fever—should see a doctor and begin treatment immediately.

- Plague patients must be kept away from other people.

- Anyone who comes close to a person who has pneumonic plague should be treated with antibiotics right away.

## Tracking Plague Today

- The U.S. Public Health Service requires that all suspected plague cases be reported to government officials.

- The United States and other countries report suspected cases of plague to the World Health Organization (WHO), which tracks plague worldwide.

- When new cases of plague are reported, the WHO often sends staff to investigate. The WHO can help local doctors diagnose plague and treat victims.

- The Centers for Disease Control and Prevention (CDC) in Fort Collins, Colorado, investigates outbreaks worldwide. They also monitor prairie dog towns, which often face another form of the disease called sylvatic plague. This disease can wipe out large groups of these animals as well as spread to humans as bubonic plague.

In the United States today, plague is most commonly spread by fleas carried by ground squirrels.

# Glossary

**antibiotics** (*an*-ti-bye-OT-iks) medicines used to stop the growth of disease-causing bacteria

**bacteria** (bac-TIHR-ee-uh) tiny living things that differ structurally from plants and animals; most bacteria are harmless, while about 100 types are known to cause disease

**biologist** (bye-OL-uh-jist) a scientist who studies living things

**buboes** (BYOO-bohz) large, painful swellings under the skin; a symptom of bubonic plague

**bubonic plague** (byoo-BON-ik PLAYG) a form of plague that occurs when plague bacteria affect the lymph nodes

**catapults** (KAT-uh-*puhlts*) ancient devices used to hurl large rocks or other objects

**contagious** (kuhn-TAY-juhss) spreading easily from one person to another

**digestive systems** (dye-JESS-tiv SISS-tuhmz) the group of organs in people or animals that help break down food so the body can use it for fuel

**fleas** (FLEEZ) small insects that live in an animal's fur

**host** (HOHST) a live plant or animal that disease-causing bacteria grow on

**lymph nodes** (LIMF NOHDZ) small masses of tissue throughout the body that help fight diseases

**mainland** (MAYN-luhnd) the largest land mass of a country

**outbreak** (OUT-*brake*) a sudden start of something, such as the spreading of a contagious disease

**pandemic** (pan-DEM-ik) an outbreak of a disease that occurs over a huge area and affects a large number of people

**plague** (PLAYG) a deadly disease spread by fleas and rodents such as rats

**pneumonic plague** (noo-MAH-nik PLAYG) a form of plague that occurs when plague bacteria settle in the lungs

**population** (*pop*-yuh-LAY-shuhn) the total number of people living in a place

**port** (PORT) a place where ships load and unload goods

**quarantined** (KWOR-uhn-teend) separated from other people in order to prevent the spread of disease

**saliva** (suh-LYE-vah) the liquid in the mouths of humans and animals that helps them swallow and chew and protects teeth against decay

**septicemic plague** (*sep*-ti-SEE-mik PLAYG) a form of plague that occurs when plague bacteria settle in the blood

**symptoms** (SIMP-tuhmz) signs of a disease—often feelings of pain or discomfort

**trade routes** (TRADE ROOTS) roads, paths, or oceans traveled by merchants bringing goods from one country to another

# Bibliography

**Kelly, John.** *The Great Mortality: An Intimate History of the Black Death, the Most Devastating Plague of All Time.* New York: Harper Perennial (2005).

www.cdc.gov/ncidod/dvbid/plague/index.htm

www.who.int/topics/plague/en/

# Read More

**Lynette, Rachel.** *Understanding Diseases and Disorders: Bubonic Plague.* San Diego, CA: KidHaven Press (2004).

**Slavicek, Louise Chipley.** *The Black Death.* New York: Chelsea House Publications (2008).

**Whiting, Jim.** *Bubonic Plague.* Hockessin, DE: Mitchell Lane Publishers (2006).

# Learn More Online

To learn more about plague, visit
**www.bearportpublishing.com/NightmarePlagues**

# Index

# About the Author

Stephen Person has written many children's books about history, science, and the environment. He lives with his family in Brooklyn, New York.